by Denise Lewis Patrick
illustrated by Steffi Walthall

Ready-to-Read

Simon Spotlight
New York London Toronto Sydney New Delhi

SIMON SPOTLIGHT
An imprint of Simon & Schuster Children's Publishing Division
1230 Avenue of the Americas, New York, New York 10020
This Simon Spotlight edition December 2021

For information about special discounts for bulk purchases, please contact Simon & Schuster Special Sales at 1-866-506-1949 or business@simonandschuster.com.
Manufactured in the United States of America 1121 LAK
2 4 6 8 10 9 7 5 3 1
CIP data for this book is available from the Library of Congress.
ISBN 978-1-6659-0788-0 (hc)
ISBN 978-1-6659-0787-3 (pbk)
ISBN 978-1-6659-0789-7 (ebook)

CONTENTS

Introduction

Have you ever felt upset when you saw someone treated unfairly? Were you brave enough to do something to help?

You should meet John Lewis.

When John was a small boy, he cared for the chickens on his family farm. His family didn't believe the chickens were very smart, but John thought they were as special as any other animals. He cared, even when no one else did.

As John grew up, he cared about how people were treated too. He spoke out about laws that treated African Americans unfairly. He was brave enough to get into what he called "good trouble" to change those laws.

Once you meet him, you'll see how he went from that small Alabama farm to the halls of the United States Congress and changed the world for the better.

Chapter 1
The Boy from Troy

John Robert Lewis was born on February 21, 1940. His parents lived on a farm near Troy, Alabama. He was the third oldest of ten children.

John's parents were sharecropper farmers, which means they rented someone else's land and used it to grow crops, but had to pay the landowners a share of the money they earned from selling the crops at harvest time. Often the landowners were not fair to the sharecropper farmers. Sometimes the farmers earned little or nothing after all their hard work.

Even as a young boy, John felt this was not right.

John's father saved money for years to buy his *own* farm. When he finally bought a farm, the farmhouse on the land didn't have running water or electricity, or an indoor bathroom. Even so, John's mother told him it was good for people to have something they can call their own.

There was plenty of work to do. John and his brothers and sisters had to help out.

John's first job on the farm, at just five years old, was taking care of the chickens. He fed them and collected their eggs. He cared about the baby chicks. John loved those chickens so much that he began to talk to them. He even gave them names! He told them Bible stories, and sometimes sounded like the pastor at church.

His family thought John might become a preacher himself when he grew up.

But soon he had another job on the farm: working in the fields, picking cotton. He did not like it and often complained to his parents about the hard work. His parents said that farm families needed everyone to work at picking time—even if it meant that John would have to miss school for days.

John didn't like missing school. So he hid at picking time. When the bus came, he hopped onto it and went to school anyway. His father was not pleased, but he let John continue going to school.

At school John learned about the world from his teachers. He learned to enjoy reading and speaking in front of the class. John's family didn't have many books at home, so he went to find more at the library.

That's when he discovered that he could not check out books from the public library in Troy. The library—like many other places in Troy and the rest of the

South—was segregated. This means that African Americans and white Americans were kept apart. African Americans went to separate schools and lived in separate neighborhoods from white Americans—and the Troy Public Library was for whites only. Some laws, called Jim Crow laws, allowed hotels, restaurants, and stores to refuse to serve African American people. Those same laws also made it difficult and dangerous for African American citizens living in Southern states to vote.

John knew segregation was wrong. By the time he was in high school, he began to dream of changing things. He just didn't know how. Then two events gave him hope.

In 1954 the US Supreme Court ruled that school segregation was unlawful and had to end.

One night a year later, he heard an amazing young minister on the radio. It was the first time John had ever heard a preacher speak about ending the unfair treatment—or injustice—that so many African Americans faced in their lives every day.

That preacher was Dr. Martin Luther King Jr.

Chapter 2
Good Trouble and Freedom Riders

John was inspired by Dr. King's message of peaceful protests and his work as a preacher. After high school John enrolled in school to become a preacher in Nashville, Tennessee. His parents didn't have money to pay for his college, so in between classes John washed dishes and cleaned rooms at his school.

"Don't get into trouble," his mother told him, but John wanted to join Dr. King's new civil rights movement. He wanted to make sure that all people were treated equally, no matter what race, gender, or religion they were. John wrote to the preacher. Dr. King sent John a bus ticket and asked him to come to Montgomery.

Dr. King's lawyer and another pastor were there in the office when eighteen-year-old John arrived. He was nervous.

Dr. King smiled and got up from his desk. "Are you the boy from Troy?" he asked.

John relaxed. He told them that he wanted to help end segregation. The older men explained that even nonviolent protests could be dangerous. Civil rights protesters could get arrested. They might be hurt. Even their families might be attacked. John listened carefully. He had a lot to think about.

Back in Nashville, John met many other students who were eager to be a part of the civil rights movement.

John and his friends knew that Jim Crow laws might be changing, but many people in the South weren't. He was willing to get into the kind of trouble that Dr. King had warned him about, because he believed this "good trouble" could change the world.

John organized sit-in protests at segregated lunch counters right in downtown Nashville. A sit-in protest is when people sit in the seats or on the floor of a business or other place and refuse to move, to show that they don't agree with practices such as segregation.

John and a group of students walked into a lunch counter and sat down. The waitress refused to serve them because they were African American. She asked them to leave. They didn't. They sat for hours. Finally, rather than serve the students, the owner closed the lunch counter.

The next day and the next, the students went to different lunch counters around the city. No one served them, but the protests got attention.

Crowds gathered. The students were called ugly names. White people threw food and spat at them. John's group followed the rules that they had learned in their nonviolent training.

Be friendly at all times. Sit up straight and face the counter. Don't hold conversations. Don't strike back if attacked.

Some students were dragged off their stools and beaten. Although they did not fight back, police came—and arrested *them*.

This was the first time John went to jail, but it wouldn't be his last. Back in Troy, his parents were not happy. His mother was afraid for him, and afraid for the family.

But the sit-ins showed John that peaceful protest could work.

After several months of protests, Nashville officials agreed to open up their lunch counters to everyone. Then John heard about another desegregation plan.

It was called the Freedom Rides.

The US Supreme Court had ruled that train and bus stations in every state had to allow all Americans to enter freely. There couldn't be any more WHITES ONLY signs for waiting rooms, bathrooms, or water fountains.

John became one of hundreds of men, women, and teenagers who tested the new law. They came from many backgrounds and over forty states. The Freedom Riders rode buses into towns across Alabama, Mississippi, and Louisiana.

They were not welcomed or wanted. They were attacked by white citizens and by police. They were pulled out of bus stations. One of their buses was even set on fire. Freedom Riders were thrown into jail again and again.

John Lewis thought of the journey as riding one step closer to freedom. By 1963 he had graduated from the seminary. But he was no longer planning to be a minister. He had chosen his life's work. He had chosen good trouble. He called it "necessary trouble."

WE EMAND
AN END TO BIAS NOW!
WE MARCH
AN END TO POLICE BRUTALITY NOW!
FREEDO
NOW
CORE

Chapter 3
Peaceful Protest

When John was twenty-three, he still believed in the idea of peaceful protest. He became the leader of a group called the Student Nonviolent Coordinating Committee (SNCC, pronounced "SNICK"). The civil rights movement had been successful in many ways, yet there was still a big problem. There was no national law to protect African Americans' rights. John decided to work with his friend Dr. King.

Dr. King and others in the movement wanted the president, John F. Kennedy, to encourage Congress to pass such a law.

John became the youngest member of a group of leaders called the Big Six, who planned a huge peaceful protest march in Washington, DC. They hoped that this march would show the president and Congress how many Americans believed that this law was necessary. Many people would speak out for equal rights that day, and John was one of them.

On August 28, 1963, more than two hundred thousand people marched to the area in Washington, DC, called the National Mall. The long day was filled with performances by famous musicians and singers; speeches by politicians and civil rights activists; and later, Martin Luther King Jr.

But before Dr. King came young John Lewis. The night before the march, the older leaders had asked John to rewrite his speech because they felt some of his words were too strong.

John argued. He finally agreed to change his speech just before he gave it, but he still sounded very much like a preacher when he stood up on the steps of the Lincoln Memorial. He told the crowd, "We are tired. . . . We want our freedom, and we want it now!"

After the march, President Kennedy and Congress worked to pass a Civil Rights Act. However, President Kennedy was assassinated—killed—only three months later, in November. It was Lyndon B. Johnson, the next president, who signed the law in 1964. This meant it was against

the law for states to treat people unfairly based on their race.

However, some Southern states continued to make life difficult for African Americans. They made it especially hard for African Americans to vote.

Chapter 4
The Edmund Pettus Bridge

Alabama, Mississippi, and other states forced African Americans to take tests or pay extra taxes before they could even register to vote. The homes and jobs of African American voters were threatened. So John and SNCC, along with Dr. King's group, the SCLC (Southern Christian Leadership Conference), decided to lead another protest. This time they planned a peaceful march from Selma, Alabama, to the state capitol in Montgomery.

The governor of Alabama supported segregation. He claimed the march was against the law, which it was not, and ordered state police to stop the event.

On March 7, 1965, John and his friend Hosea Williams of SCLC led six hundred marchers. The people linked arms and sang before they started across the Edmund Pettus Bridge in Selma. They walked two by two on the sidewalk, even though the bridge was closed to traffic.

When they reached the other side, state

police and others told them to turn back. When the protestors did not move, dozens of state policemen—along with armed citizens working with sheriff's deputies—rushed at them on foot. Men on horseback carried clubs and other weapons. John was struck in the head so hard that his skull was cracked.

Reporters from several US newspapers and TV stations were in Selma to cover the protests. News photographers captured photos of the bloody protestors trying to get to safety, including several photos of the state trooper attacking John. That picture, and others of the violence, made news around the world.

The day became known as Bloody Sunday. When President Johnson saw what had happened, he called on Congress to pass a Voting Rights Act. They did, only months later, in August 1965.

Chapter 5
The "Conscience of Congress"

John recovered from his injuries on Bloody Sunday. He left SNCC in 1966. In 1967 he met a smart librarian in Atlanta named Lillian Miles. She helped him through one of the saddest days of his life, when his friend Dr. King was assassinated in 1968. From the day they married later that year, Lillian was his closest adviser.

John Lewis spent much of the 1970s working with the Voter Education Project. Once again he was helping people register to vote, and to understand their civil rights. John decided he might help people even more if he became a member of the US Congress. So he ran for election to the

House of Representatives in 1986. With the support and votes of many Georgians whom his work had helped, John won! He became a congressman.

In Congress, John Lewis continued to be an activist, speaking up for poor people, education, voting rights, and equality. John was respected by other members of Congress for the dangerous and hard work he had done in the 1960s. In 2016 he participated in one more sit-in—on the floor of Congress—to help call for gun-control laws. He became known as "the conscience of Congress."

His lifetime of work for justice and equal rights made him famous around the world. President Barack Obama awarded him the Presidential Medal of Freedom in 2011. It is the highest civilian (not military) award that any American can receive.

In 2016, John also won a National Book Award for Young People's Literature for helping to write a series of graphic novels about his life. He received the award for the third book in the series, *March: Book Three*. In a speech, he almost cried as he recalled not being able to check out books from the Troy Public Library when he was a boy. Like many other hardships in his life, that did not stop John Lewis. "I tried to read everything!" he said.

After serving seventeen terms as a US Representative for the state of Georgia, John Robert Lewis died of cancer on July 17, 2020. His bravery and his determination to cause "good trouble, necessary trouble" forever changed America and its people.

BUT WAIT . . .

THERE'S MORE!

Turn the page to find out how to get into good trouble, learn about other activists from around the world, and more!

Getting Into Good Trouble

Is there an issue that you feel passionate about? Have you thought of taking action and encouraging others to do the same? John Lewis believed in making change through nonviolent methods. Here are some ways to peacefully take action in your community:

Contact your local US Representative— Let your concerns be heard by those who represent you in government. Talk to a trusted grown-up about how to reach out.

Make signs or buttons—Make issues visible by making signs or buttons that people can see.

Speak up—If you notice someone saying or doing something that doesn't respect another person's rights, tell a trusted grown-up so you can find a way to help together.

Volunteer—Find a local group or organization related to the cause you're passionate about and volunteer to help raise awareness at events. Look for small actions you can take in your neighborhood or town.

Keep learning—Stay active in and educated about the cause you believe in so you can be a good spokesperson for it.

Listen—Always listen to the people whose rights you're fighting for, and support them in finding ways to share their own voices.

Activist Heroes

John Lewis joined the civil rights movement and fought for equality for African Americans. There are many other civil rights leaders around the world. These are just a few of them:

Diane Nash is a civil rights leader who helped keep the Freedom Riders going after the first thirteen Freedom Riders were arrested.

Deborah Parker, or **Tsi-Cy-Altsa,** is an American Indian activist in the United States. She has fought for the rights of American Indians to govern themselves, for protections for American Indian women, for environmental justice, and more.

Malala Yousafzai is an activist who fights for allowing women and children in Pakistan and many other countries to receive free, safe access to education. At seventeen years old she was the youngest person to ever receive the Nobel Peace Prize.

Menaka Guruswamy and **Arundhati Katju** are two lawyers in India who successfully overturned a law that made it a crime to love someone of the same gender.

Bernard Lafayette is a civil rights activist and was a leader during the civil rights movement. A friend of John Lewis, Bernard also led sit-ins, took part in the Freedom Rides, and helped organize the Selma-to-Montgomery marches that resulted in the Voting Rights Act of 1965.

Venerable Pomnyun Sunim is a Korean Buddhist monk and social activist known for working to feed the hungry, cure the sick, educate children, and more.

Rights for All

Activists fight for many types of human rights all over the world, including rights that American citizens have and sometimes take for granted.

For example, children in the United States have the right to an education, but there are children in some parts of the world who are not allowed to attend school or who do not have access to education, such as learning to read and write. This can affect their ability to make a living when they grow up, and more.

Can you think of some rights that you have that others may not have, or may not have as fully? Ask a grown-up what you can do to help, and maybe someday you will be a part of making things better.

Running for Congress

John Lewis became a congressman when he was elected to the United States House of Representatives. Congress is one branch of the United States government. It is called the legislative branch and is the part of government with the power to write and vote on laws for the country, among other things.

If you want to run for the US House of Representatives someday like John Lewis, you have to:

- be at least twenty-five years old.
- have been a citizen of the United States for at least seven years.
- live in the state you wish to represent.

We believe in you!

Meanwhile, if you hear about a law you don't agree with or an issue that needs attention in your community, you can talk to a trusted grown-up about reaching out to your US representative by writing a letter, sending an email, or making a phone call to talk about it and share your opinion.

Now that you've met John Lewis, what have you learned?

1. What kind of farmer was John's father when John was very young?
a. a sharecropper b. a sharefarmer c. a farmsharer

2. What was John's first job?
a. US Representative b. working at a lunch counter
c. feeding chickens

3. What is the name for a peaceful protest that involves sitting down at a business or other place in order to exercise your rights and express your beliefs?
a. stand-down protest b. sit-in protest c. walk-out protest

4. What was Dr. Martin Luther King Jr.'s name for John Lewis?
a. the Boy from Selma b. the Good Trouble Boy
c. the Boy from Troy

5. What did John Lewis want to be when he was in college?
a. a preacher b. a farmer c. a poet

6. What was the name of the group of protestors who rode buses to protest segregation?
a. Bus Riders b. Freedom Riders c. Protest Riders

7. What kind of rights were John Lewis and other protestors trying to call attention to by crossing the Edmund Pettus Bridge?
a. voting rights b. human rights c. animal rights

8. What did John's father let him do instead of picking cotton in picking season?
a. go to bed b. go to school c. go to the candy store

9. What kind of trouble did John Lewis believe in?
a. good trouble b. necessary trouble
c. both a and b

10. What did John become known as, in Congress?
a. the mind of Congress b. the heart of Congress
c. the conscience of Congress

Answers: 1.a 2.c 3.b 4.c 5.a 6.b 7.a 8.b 9.c 10.c

REPRODUCIBLE